The Quotation Bank for A-Level

Hamlet

William Shakespeare

Copyright © 2022 Esse Publishing Limited and Nikki Carlin
The moral rights of the authors have been asserted.

First published in 2022 by:
The Quotation Bank
Esse Publishing Limited
10 9 8 7 6 5 4 3 2 1

All rights reserved. No part of this publication may be reproduced, resold, stored in a retrieval system or transmitted in any form, or by any means (electronic, photocopying, mechanical or otherwise) without the prior written permission of both the copyright owners and the publisher.

A CIP catalogue record for this book is available from the British Library.
ISBN 978-1-9999816-6-2

All enquiries to: contact@thequotationbank.co.uk
Every effort has been made to trace and contact all relevant copyright holders. However, if contacted the publisher will rectify any omission or error at the earliest opportunity.

Printed and bound by Target Print Limited, Broad Lane, Cottenham, Cambridge CB24 8SW.

www.thequotationbank.co.uk

Introduction

How The Quotation Bank can help you in your exams	4
How to use The Quotation Bank	5

Quotations

Act One	6
Act Two	11
Act Three	16
Act Four	21
Act Five	26
Critical and Contextual Quotations	31

Revision and Essay Planning

Performance History	41
How to revise effectively	42
Suggested revision activities	43
Glossary	44

Welcome to The Quotation Bank, the comprehensive guide to all the key quotations you need to succeed in your exams.

Whilst you may have read the play, watched a film adaptation, understood the plot and have a strong grasp of context, all questions in your A-Levels require you to write a focused essay, full of textual references and quotations (be they textual, critical or contextual), and most importantly, quotations that you then analyse.

I think we all agree it is **analysis** that is the tricky part – and that is why we are here to help!

The Quotation Bank takes 25 of the most important quotations from the text, interprets them, analyses them, highlights literary techniques Shakespeare has used, puts them in context, and suggests which quotations you might use in which essays. We have also included 10 contextual and critical quotations, analysed them, and linked them closely to the text, all for you to explore.

At the end of **The Quotation Bank** we have put together a performance history and great revision exercises to help you prepare for your exam. We have also included a detailed glossary to make sure you completely understand what certain literary terms actually mean!

How The Quotation Bank can help you in your exams.

The Quotation Bank is designed to make sure every point you make in an essay clearly fulfils the Assessment Objectives an examiner will be using when marking your work.

Every quotation comes with the following detailed material:

Interpretation: The interpretation of each quotation allows you to fulfil **AO1**, articulating an informed, personal response, and **AO5**, using different interpretations to inform your exploration of the text.

Techniques: Using associated concepts and terminology (in this case, the techniques used by Shakespeare) is a key part of **AO1**, and can help you identify and analyse ways in which meanings are shaped (**AO2**).

Analysis: We have provided as much analysis (**AO2**) as possible, as well as exploring the significance and influence of contextual material (**AO3**) and different interpretations (**AO5**). It is a great idea to analyse the quotation in detail – you need to do more than just say what it means, but also try to explore a variety of different ways of interpreting it.

Use in essays on… Your answer needs to be focused to fulfil **AO1**. This section helps you choose relevant quotations and link them together for a stronger, more detailed essay.

How to use The Quotation Bank.

Many students spend time learning quotations by heart. This can be useful, but it is important to remember what you are meant to do with quotations once you get into the exam.

By using **The Quotation Bank**, not only will you have a huge number of textual, critical and contextual quotations to use in your essays, you will also have ideas on what to say about them, how to analyse them, how to link them together, and what questions to use them for.

These quotations can form the basis of your answer, making sure every point articulates an informed, personal response **(AO1)** and allows you to analyse ways in which meanings are shaped **(AO2)**.

The critical and contextual quotations allow you to easily and effectively explore the significance and influence of context **(AO3)**, and provide you with a variety of different readings to explore **(AO5).**

The textual quotations cover the whole text to allow you to show comprehensive whole text knowledge, and the critical and contextual quotations cover the full range of the text's publication history to help you explore the contexts in which the text was both written and received **(AO3)**.

Act One Scene Two:

HAMLET: "Oh that this too solid flesh would melt,/ thaw and resolve itself into a dew/ or that the Everlasting had not fixed/ His canon 'gainst self-slaughter. Oh God, God."

Interpretation: In Hamlet's first soliloquy the audience learn he is truly unhappy. This is the first time he admits he is contemplating suicide; he knows it is a great sin and so is in despair.

Techniques: Metaphor; Repetition.

Analysis:

- In some versions of the play "solid" is "sullied", implying Hamlet feels tainted or spoiled in some way, and he feels inadequate. Either way, he wishes to no longer be alive, for his physical self to "melt" into the earth.
- The play is set in a Christian world, in which suicide or "self-slaughter" is a sin. Hamlet declares his religious belief is the only thing holding him back but as the play continues we learn he often chooses inaction over action.
- Repetition of "Oh God, God" stresses Hamlet's pain and emotional torment over the death of his father and rapid re-marriage of his mother to Claudius.

Use in essays on…Religion; Action Vs Inaction; Death and Decay.

Act One Scene Two:
HAMLET: "Frailty – thy name is Woman."

Interpretation: Hamlet is angry at his mother for being disloyal and weak by agreeing to marry Claudius. His anger is not just aimed at his mother, but at all women.

Techniques: Personification; Metaphor; Foreshadowing.

Analysis:
- Hamlet is implying Gertrude is morally weak and disloyal because of her hasty marriage to Claudius. However, this also foreshadows his later opinion of Ophelia, and by extension, all women. He feels frequently let down by the women he loves for betraying him.
- Both Hamlet and his father's ghost imply that Gertrude's "frailty" is symbolised by her marrying Claudius because of lust. Her weakness is considered a sinful act when she should have been a grieving widow.
- Hamlet believes women personify "frailty", a weakness of body and mind, a typically misogynistic attitude of the period. Shakespeare reinforces this idea as Ophelia is introduced and quickly seen as a character who does not express her own mind.

Use in essays on… Relationships and Sexuality; Role of Women.

Act One Scene Three:
> **OPHELIA:** "I do not know, my Lord, what I should think."

Interpretation: Ophelia's response to her father is typically empty of emotion or honesty; from the outset she is established as a character who is obedient to her father and rarely seems to act on her own thoughts or feelings.

Techniques: Language.

Analysis:
- This statement sums up Ophelia's passive attitude for the first half of the play; the simple, monosyllabic language suggests she has very little to say. Ophelia seems to have no voice of her own, obeying all orders given to her by the men in her life, rarely expressing her true feelings until she goes mad.
- Some critics argue Ophelia and Hamlet have a sexual relationship; Ophelia's uncertain response may be due to her wanting to hide the truth from Polonius. However, it may suggest she is naïve, unsure how to respond to Hamlet's love.
- She shows respect to her father, addressing him as "my Lord", and ending the scene saying she will "obey" him. We are left wondering what Ophelia really thinks about being ordered to stay away from Hamlet. If she is in love with him this must be very painful for her to do, yet she obeys without question.

Use in essays on… Role of Women; Relationships and Sexuality; Appearance Vs Reality.

Act One Scene Four:
> MARCELLUS: "Something is rotten in the state of Denmark."

Interpretation: Marcellus, upon seeing the Ghost, is worried it signals a bad omen or trouble for the country. There is a sense of uncertainty and unease in his statement, setting the tone for the indecision and confusion that is threaded throughout the play.

Techniques: Imagery; Metaphor; Adjective.

Analysis:
- "Rotten" has connotations of decay, disease, and poison – images which occur frequently throughout the play. Shakespeare uses "rotten" to imply Marcellus believes there is corruption and immorality in Claudius' court and that the Ghost is a bad omen.
- "State" could be interpreted in two ways; the country of Denmark itself, or the condition of the country. Claudius' sinful behaviour, such as his rapid marriage to Gertrude and the excessive drinking he encourages at court, have begun to eat away at Denmark's reputation and spread like a disease.
- The vague nature of "something" not only implies an uncertainty about what may come, but a reluctance to suggest who is responsible for these unhappy events: the King.

Use in essays on…Morality; Corruption; Death and Decay.

Act One Scene Five:
  GHOST: "Won to his shameful lust/the will of my most seeming virtuous Queen."

Interpretation: The Ghost condemns both Gertrude and Claudius for marrying so soon after his murder, suggesting Gertrude was tempted by Claudius' appearance and that their marriage is based on nothing but "lust". They are both cast as sinners.

Techniques: Adjective; Juxtaposition; Foreshadowing.

Analysis:
- In Act 1 Scene 2 Hamlet takes offence when Gertrude suggests he "seems" unhappy, saying "nay it is, I know not 'seems'". The Ghost is implying that Gertrude's virtue when he was alive was simply an act; she was "seeming" to be an honourable Queen but was very quickly disloyal after his death.
- The Ghost's description of Claudius' and Gertrude's relationship as "shameful lust" echoes Hamlet's earlier comment about "incestuous sheets". Their marriage is considered sinful by both, but this could imply the Ghost is merely echoing Hamlet's own thoughts in order to lure him into taking revenge.
- The juxtaposition of the adjectives "shameful" and "virtuous" not only describe Gertrude but also foreshadow Ophelia's downfall and the reasons why Polonius and Laertes warn her to stay away from Hamlet.

Use in essays on…Appearance Vs Reality; Role of Women; Relationships and Sexuality.

Act Two Scene One:
> **POLONIUS: "By indirections, find directions out."**

Interpretation: Polonius reveals his cunning and sly character by instructing a spy to find out information about his son in a devious manner.

Techniques: Paradox; Foreshadowing.

Analysis:
- Polonius' paradoxical order, "by indirections, find indirections out", reveals he is an underhand, deceitful character who would rather manipulatively sneak around to find the information he needs than be direct.
- This mirrors Claudius, who employs Hamlet's friends to observe him and report back. Polonius sinks to disturbing levels in order to help the king by utilising his own daughter as bait in their desire to find out what Hamlet is thinking.
- Polonius' words foreshadow many key moments in the play and the recurrence of characters being deceptive to achieve their aims. Hamlet is also guilty of using this approach by employing the group of actors to perform 'The Mousetrap' and "catch the conscience of the king".

Use in essays on… Appearance Vs Reality; Morality; Corruption.

Act Two Scene One:
   OPHELIA: "As if he had been loosed out of hell/to speak of horrors."
Interpretation: Ophelia expresses fear and concern for Hamlet after having seen his recent frantic behaviour and dishevelled appearance. It is the first time the audience hear of him acting with true madness.
Techniques: Imagery; Simile; Dramatic Irony.
Analysis:
- Ophelia unknowingly uses similar language to that used to describe the ghost in Act One, which could foreshadow a grim ending for Hamlet if the audience now hear of him resembling his dead father. The simile of him being "loosed out of hell" is also ironic for the audience who know that King Hamlet claimed to have been trapped in purgatory.
- "Hell' and "horrors" allude to sin and evil, implying Hamlet is tormented by the immorality of Claudius and Gertrude. Some critics argue his torment could be a result of his own sin with Ophelia; her rejection of him has led to his madness.
- Until now Hamlet's insanity has been almost jester-like, fooling and teasing others. Ophelia's imagery leads the audience to wonder; is he really mad with grief and rejection, or is he playing a part, knowing she will report his behaviour to her father and the king?

Use in essays on… Appearance Vs Reality; Madness; Religion.

Act Two Scene Two:
> HAMLET: "Excellent well, you are a fishmonger."

Interpretation: Hamlet is pretending to be mad by implying he doesn't know Polonius, assuming he is a lowly "fishmonger"; however, his use of a pun to insult Polonius highlights to the audience that he is in complete control of his mind.

Techniques: Pun; Irony.

Analysis:
- Many critics and audiences assert Hamlet knows about Polonius' plan to use Ophelia to entrap him and discover the real reason for his change in behaviour. The word "fishmonger" was a play on the word 'fleshmonger', a 16th century term for a brothel keeper. Hamlet is calling out Polonius for using his daughter as a tool in his immoral games.
- Hamlet frequently teases Polonius with comments and insults that the elder statesman does not appear to notice. The audience see Hamlet's mind is sharp and witty in mocking Polonius by acting as if he does not know who he is.
- Polonius is made out to be not only a figure of fun, but in using his daughter in this way, Hamlet is also highlighting his corrupt and deceitful side.

Use in essays on… Madness; Role of Women; Appearance Vs Reality.

Act Two Scene Two:
>   HAMLET: "Why it/appeareth nothing to me, but a foul and pestilent/ congregation of vapours."

Interpretation: Hamlet, looking at the night sky, can see no beauty or hope in the world anymore. Where there was once beauty, he now sees corruption, death, and sin.

Techniques: Metaphor; Juxtaposition; Adjective.

Analysis:
- The religious metaphor of the sky being a "congregation" alongside the adjectives "foul" and "pestilent" juxtapose the ideas of morality and sin. A gathering of devoted and faithful people has now become a corrupt world where he is surrounded by people he cannot trust.
- "Foul" and "pestilent" have connotations of death, disease, rot, and disgust. Hamlet's Denmark is not only rotten at its core with regards the king, but Hamlet believes it spreads and infects others. This is particularly important since he is addressing his friends who have been persuaded to spy on him and report back to Claudius, therefore also becoming infected by his immorality.
- The word "nothing" appears repeatedly in the play and emphasises Hamlet's nihilistic attitude. He feels life has no value anymore.

Use in essays on…Death and Decay; Morality; Corruption; Madness.

Act Two Scene Two:
> HAMLET: "Yet I, a dull and muddy mettled rascal, peak/like John-a-dreams, unpregnant of my cause,/ and can say nothing."

Interpretation: Hamlet berates himself for not acting to avenge his father's murder. He compares himself to a blunt sword, inactive, confused and weak.

Techniques: Metaphor; Simile; Imagery; Soliloquy.

Analysis:
- "Dull" means blunt, like a weapon that cannot injure, or slow to act; Hamlet feels both here. "Muddy mettled" also suggests muddled and lacking resilience, reinforcing the suggestion Hamlet is confused and lacks the courage to act.
- Hamlet feels shame he has not acted on his intentions; he is "unpregnant", implying he is unresponsive to his cause. This is an interesting choice of vocabulary; Hamlet's cause is to kill Claudius and therefore raises the moral question of taking a life. Has Hamlet lost sight of right and wrong because he is infected by the corruption in Denmark?
- The repeated motif of "nothing" reminds us of Hamlet's desire to kill himself as he feels worthless. The audience may also note Shakespeare chooses "say nothing" instead of "do nothing", reinforcing Hamlet's inability to take action.

Use in essays on… Action Vs Inaction; Morality; Corruption; Revenge.

Act Three Scene One:
   HAMLET: "Or, to take arms against a sea of troubles,/and by opposing end them."

Interpretation: Hamlet contemplates life and how to endure living with an unbearable "sea of troubles". He wonders if it might be better to fight the troubles he faces or simply "end them".

Techniques: Metaphor; Paradox; Soliloquy.

Analysis:
- Hamlet's mixed metaphor suggests the futility of trying to fight against the corruption that surrounds him. The imagery of him fighting against an unstoppable "sea of troubles" implies he is being overwhelmed by these "troubles", and could also indicate that he is in danger ("take arms").
- The paradoxical nature of this metaphor underlines the fact that, so far, Hamlet has been unable to act and carry out his intentions to avenge his father. He seems frozen by inaction.
- The ambiguity of his statement leads the audience to wonder if he means to "take arms" against his worries and bring them to an end or if, in line with his previous statements, he actually means to end his life.

Use in essays on… Action Vs Inaction; Death and Decay; Morality; Revenge.

Act Three Scene Three:
> CLAUDIUS: "O, my offence is rank; it smells to heaven;/ it hath the primal eldest curse upon't -/A brother's murder."

Interpretation: Claudius is admitting that he murdered King Hamlet, and seems to be distressed at the sin ("offence") he has committed.

Techniques: Soliloquy; Allusion.

Analysis:
- By talking about his "offence", this soliloquy takes the form of a confession or a prayer. Biblical allusion to Cain killing Abel ("A brother's murder"), the first murder in the bible, stresses that Claudius is aware of the severity of his sin, yet the irony lies in his determination to continue profiting from his crime and not give up the crown.
- The language choices of "rank" and "smells" have connotations of death, disease, and corruption. He is also aware that God knows that he has sinned ("it smells to heaven") and has upset the natural order of succession. The divine right of kings has been corrupted and so Claudius, like Cain, will be cursed, as will his Kingdom.

Use in essays on…Disease; Morality; Corruption; Religion.

Act Three Scene Three:
> CLAUDIUS: "O, wretched state! O bosom black as death!"

Interpretation: Claudius, still on his knees and looking as if he is praying, is in despair as he cannot (or will not) confess his sins and ask for forgiveness properly; he does not want to lose all he has gained. He knows he is damned.

Techniques: Exclamations; Simile; Dramatic Irony.

Analysis:
- Shakespeare alludes to Marcellus' earlier comment about the rotten state of Denmark; again the meaning is ambiguous. Claudius is most likely talking about the "state" of his own soul – he is "wretched" meaning sorrowful and anguished – but as King he could also be talking about his Kingdom and the terrible danger he has inflicted upon it through his sin.
- "Bosom black as death" conveys both guilt but also selfishness; he bemoans the darkness of his "bosom" as like death, yet he inflicted death upon his brother. It is a stunning lack of awareness for others that Claudius pities himself so much.
- It is important to note that at this moment Claudius must look as if he is praying and so he should be on his knees, looking as if he is begging for forgiveness. The audience, however, know this is not the case.

Use in essays on… Disease; Morality; Corruption; Religion.

Act Three Scene Three:
> HAMLET: "Now might I do it, but now he is a-praying."

Interpretation: Hamlet is considering killing Claudius as he sees him alone and vulnerable, but quickly changes his mind when he thinks he is praying. Is Hamlet merely seeking another excuse to put off that which he feels will damn his own soul?

Techniques: Dramatic Irony.

Analysis:
- Hamlet is on the cusp of killing Claudius and taking the revenge he has long agonised over, but when he sees Claudius "praying" (or so he believes), he realises he cannot. He justifies this change of heart, explaining that if he kills Claudius in prayer then his soul will go to heaven, but the audience may wonder if this is simply another excuse for Hamlet to not carry out his actions.
- The modal verb "might" and the conjunction "but" signify Hamlet's uncertainty. The speed with which he changes his mind is also notable; within one brief sentence Shakespeare has shown us how fearful Hamlet is of commiting to his plan and killing his uncle.

Use in essays on… Revenge; Religion; Action Vs Inaction; Appearance Vs Reality.

Act Three Scene Four:
> GERTRUDE: "Thou turn'st my eyes into my very soul/and there I see such black and grieved spots/as will not leave their tinct."

Interpretation: Gertrude has been told of Claudius' crimes and has realised her own sins in trusting and marrying him. She expresses guilt and sorrow at the way she has behaved following the murder of her husband.

Techniques: Metaphor; Imagery; Adjective.

Analysis:
- Hamlet has forced Gertrude to metaphorically look inwards and reflect on her actions since the death of the King. It is as if, until this moment, she has not had to take any responsibility for herself and has always followed the example set by each husband. Even here, it is her son who makes her change her mind and so the audience wonder if, like Ophelia, Gertrude has her own mind at all.
- "Black and grieved spots" echo Claudius' description of his own soul as "black as death". Gertrude seems innocent of any involvement in the murder but her complicity in the marriage so soon after her husband's death leaves her feeling she too has sinned. In some versions of the play "grieved" becomes "grained"; both imply a lasting reminder of the death and pain that has been caused.

Use in essays on… Death and Decay; Religion; Morality; Corruption; Role of Women.

Act Four Scene Three:
CLAUDIUS: "For like the hectic in my blood he rages/And thou must cure me."

Interpretation: Claudius needs to take swift action against Hamlet by sending him to England to be killed. Claudius is realising the consequences of not only killing the king, but also encouraging Hamlet to stay in Denmark and believing he could control him.

Techniques: Simile; Personification; Soliloquy.

Analysis:
- Hamlet is compared to a "hectic", meaning a poison or disease that has infected Claudius. This implies Hamlet's recent behaviour has caused Claudius to be overwhelmed and sick with worry that he is going to be found out. Also, the King represents the country so the audience can infer that the "hectic" is infecting Denmark too.
- Claudius calls on England to "cure" him, using the semantic field of disease to reinforce the idea that sin and corruption are rife in Denmark.
- The personification of the disease through the verb "rages" indicates how much of a worry Hamlet is for Claudius, implying he believes Hamlet to be dangerous and violent.

Use in essays on…Death and Decay; Action Vs Inaction; Revenge.

Act Four Scene Four:
> HAMLET: "O, from this time forth/my thoughts be bloody or be nothing worth."

Interpretation: Hamlet vows to take action against Claudius, frustrated with himself for not having yet taken revenge; he promises to think of nothing else from now on.

Techniques: Metaphor; Motif.

Analysis:
- The use of the noun "thoughts" instead of "actions" continues to reinforce the idea that Hamlet is permanently stuck in a state of inaction. The metaphor of his thoughts being "bloody" merely suggests he will think of and plan his revenge, yet the audience still wonder if he will actually kill the king.
- The adjective "bloody" reminds the audience of Hamlet's rash actions when he murdered Polonius. He is capable of acting violently on impulse which may foreshadow things to come.
- The motif of "nothing" is repeated here, implying that in the end Hamlet's actions may not lead to any satisfaction or redemption. The audience are constantly reminded of the futility of revenge.

Use in essays on…Action Vs Inaction; Revenge.

Act Four Scene Five:
> OPHELIA: "I cannot choose but weep to think they would lay him/i' th' cold ground."

Interpretation: Ophelia is grieving for her father, distressed not only at his death but his simple and uncremonious funeral in the "cold ground".

Techniques: Language.

Analysis:
- Ophelia, in her madness, is finally able to speak freely and without the worry of dishonouring herself or her family. In one of her few prose lines in this scene, Ophelia expresses her true feelings for perhaps the first time as she grieves for Polonius.
- Her language is passive as she declares she will do nothing "but weep". Despite her new openness, she is still characterised as a passive character who is acted upon rather than someone who takes action – she "cannot choose" and must wait for "they" to bury her father. She must wait for her brother to return in order for revenge to be sought for her father, and so she once again finds herself under the control of the men in her life.

Use in essays on…Madness; Role of Women; Death and Decay.

Act Four Scene Five:
> CLAUDIUS: "O, this is the poison of deep grief."

Interpretation: Claudius believes it is Ophelia's grief for her father that has driven her to insanity.

Techniques: Metaphor; Irony.

Analysis:
- Claudius believes grief for her father, Polonius, is the sole cause of Ophelia's madness. He speaks with certainty, using the declarative statement "this is" but the use of "O" at the beginning of the statement could suggest he is feeling impatient or unsettled by her behaviour. Alternatively, "O" could be an emotive expression of sympathy, especially as Gertrude seems so affected by Ophelia.
- Claudius again mentions "poison", the very weapon he used against King Hamlet. It is as if his own sins infect his thoughts constantly since he speaks a great deal about infection and decay. "Poison" being used to metaphorically describe the symptoms of grief could imply he believes grief is a dangerous emotion and one that should be cured. This would indicate a lack of sympathy for Ophelia, and reinforces the suggestion he is unsettled by her sudden honesty and lack of care.

Use in essays on...Madness; Death and Decay.

Act Four Scene Five:
> LAERTES "I'll not be juggled with./To hell allegiance, vows to the blackest devil,/Conscience and grace to the profoundest pit."

Interpretation: Laertes is angry about the murder and unceremonious burial of his father. He seeks revenge and states he will do anything ("blackest devil") to get it.

Techniques: Semantic Field; Juxtaposition; Irony.

Analysis:
- Laertes' determined tone in his desire for revenge contrasts with Hamlet's prevaricating. Laertes is a foil for Hamlet; determined where Hamlet is unsure, taking action where Hamlet merely plans. He casts aside friendship and duty to Hamlet, declaring "to hell allegiance", as avenging his father takes precedence.
- Ironically Laertes insists he "will not be juggled with" and will not be taken for a fool or manipulated. However, he allows himself to be led by Claudius who plots the murder of Hamlet in an underhand and deceptive manner.
- The semantic field of religion stresses Laertes' determination for revenge, in contrast with Hamlet. Juxtaposition of "vows", "conscience" and "grace", with "hell", "devil" and "pit" indicate how much Laertes is willing to sacrifice in order to kill Hamlet.

Use in essays on… Revenge; Religion; Action Vs Inaction; Morality.

Act Five Scene One:
 HAMLET: "To what base uses we may return, Horatio!/Why may not imagination trace the noble dust of/Alexander til he find it stopping a bung hole?"

Interpretation: Hamlet ponders the meaning of life and how all become equal in death. He reflects on the life of Alexander the Great who, in death, is reduced to ashes and clay.

Techniques: Juxtaposition; Imagery; Oxymoron.

Analysis:
- "Return" alludes to the book of Genesis in which Adam and Eve are created in clay. Hamlet suggests we all "return" to the ground, Kings and commoners, and are nothing in death. He appears to find this idea liberating rather than morbid.
- The oxymoron "noble dust" in reference to Alexander also brings to mind Hamlet's dead father – could Hamlet now be questioning the visitation from the Ghost and the power it has over him if, in death, we are nothing but "dust"?
- The juxtaposition of Alexander the Great stopping up a "bung hole" creates the almost humorous imagery of a great man reduced to nothing but a cork – a mere tool or object made from the body of a man who once conquered half the world. Hamlet's realisation signals his new confidence and understanding of who he is and how he must act. There is no more uncertainty.

Use in essays on...Death and Decay; Action Vs Inaction.

Act Five Scene One:
 LAERTES: "Lay her i' the earth,/and from her fair and unpolluted flesh/may violets spring."

Interpretation: Laertes is grieving for Ophelia and praising her for, in his eyes at least, remaining virtuous and chaste. Laertes often seems concerned with Ophelia's virginity.

Techniques: Metaphor; Imagery.

Analysis:
- Ophelia is often associated with flower imagery, and "violets" in literature are commonly associated with faithfulness, modesty, and chastity.
- "Unpolluted flesh" appears to be a rather vulgar term, reducing Ophelia to nothing but a body which was intended to remain untouched. Of course, Laertes cannot know if Ophelia's flesh is indeed "unpolluted" but given his warning to her previously, it is clear that he is overly interested in her romantic relationships. He could also be describing her this way to protect some part of her honour after she is found to have killed herself.
- "Unpolluted" also calls to mind the corruption and sin which is rife in Denmark – it is up to the audience to decide if Ophelia is an innocent victim of the manipulation and deceit that has taken place, or if she took an active part.

Use in essays on…Role of Women; Death and Decay.

Act Five Scene One:
> HAMLET: "For though I am not splenitive rash,/ yet I have in me something dangerous/ which let thy wisdom fear."

Interpretation: Hamlet warns Laertes not to underestimate him; he is dangerous and finally showing self-awareness, not prevaricating about who he is or what he should do.

Techniques: Metaphor.

Analysis:
- The ambiguity of the metaphor "something dangerous" inside Hamlet could mean he knows he is capable of murder. It is ironic however that he claims not to be "rash", considering the murder of Polonius. Hamlet could now be said to have returned to his old self and feels more in control of his actions.
- Alternatively, the danger inside Hamlet could be that he is unafraid of death. Having contemplated it for so long and realised we all must die, it is likely Hamlet is saying he will take on any fight and any challenge as he no longer has anything to live for. Interestingly, he no longer seems to be saddened by this idea. For the first time he is speaking with a tone of conviction and confidence.
- He warns Laertes to heed his advice and "fear" him, stressing he still cares for his old friend and has no quarrel with him.

Use in essays on… Revenge; Action Vs Inaction; Madness.

Act Five Scene Two:
> GERTRUDE: "I will, my lord. I pray you pardon me."

Interpretation: Gertrude defies Claudius's instruction to not drink the wine and in so doing, declares herself for Hamlet. It is unclear if she knows that she is drinking poison.

Techniques: Language.

Analysis:
- Gertrude's simple language here could indicate her determination and strength in finally defying her husband and choosing to support her son instead. In toasting Hamlet, she is declaring she is on the side of truth and justice, distancing herself from her corrupt and murderous husband.
- If Gertrude does know that the cup is poisoned then she is showing even greater courage, and perhaps also seeking redemption for her own role in the tragedy by deliberately taking her own life in order to save Hamlet's.
- Her formal language "my lord" and "pardon me", suggest that, despite knowing the truth about Claudius, Gertrude is still bound by the conventions of her role as Queen and as a wife/woman.

Use in essays on…Role of Women; Relationships and Sexuality; Morality.

Act Five Scene Two:

> HORATIO: "Now cracks a noble heart. Goodnight, sweet prince,/and flights of angels sing thee to thy rest."

Interpretation: A heartbroken Horatio says a final prayer for Hamlet. It is particularly poignant that Horatio is the only person left to mourn for him.

Techniques: Language; Metaphor.

Analysis:
- This emotive prayer for Hamlet reveals Horatio to be a true friend and someone who loved Hamlet dearly. Wishing him "goodnight", rather than goodbye, and calling him "sweet prince", makes Horatio sound more like a father figure than a friend. It is ironic that, in death, Hamlet has the father figure he has longed for.
- The metaphor of Horatio's breaking "noble heart" indicates just how sorrowful he is about Hamlet's death.
- The use of the adverb "now" implies that after all the tragedy and death he has seen, it is this moment that truly hurts.

Use in essays on…Death and Decay; Relationships and Sexuality.

Voltaire (1748) argues that,
> "[Hamlet] is a vulgar and barbarous drama."

Interpretation: Voltaire found the entire play to be distasteful and, while crediting Shakespeare with some genius, claims *Hamlet* seems to have been written by "a drunken savage".

Analysis:
- It is easy to see why Voltaire could not find anything particularly life-affirming about a play so full of corruption, murder, and deceit as *Hamlet*. However, a modern audience would have to play this against the fact *Hamlet* is one of Shakespeare's most adapted and popular plays; there must be something in all that vulgarity and barbarity which appeals to our humanity.
- On the face of it, *Hamlet* could indeed be described as "vulgar", given the presentations of Gertrude and Claudius, for example. However, it is commonly argued that the beauty of the play lies in Hamlet's own character, particularly his soliloquies. It is here that Shakespeare uses his protagonist to explore some of the great complexities of human nature, of life and death, and the nature of our relationships with one another.

Use in essays on...Morality and Corruption.

Samuel Johnson (1765) suggests that,
> "Hamlet is...rather an instrument than an agent."

Interpretation: Johnson puts forward the argument Hamlet is a victim of circumstances and the actions of other people, rather than someone who takes control of his own fate.

Analysis:
- From the outset, Hamlet is acting on the orders of his father's ghost – or rather, he is thinking about acting. He talks about "taking arms against a sea of troubles" but in fact does very little proactively to take charge of his troubling circumstances.
- The use "instrument" is interesting as it implies that Hamlet is used in some way by other characters, but this is hardly the case. Claudius and Polonius attempt to fool and manipulate him, but Hamlet is careful to play the same games in return.
- Could it be argued then that Hamlet is an instrument of fate, and of his own troubled mind? He talks about Denmark being a prison, but it could also be said that he is imprisoned by his own worries and therefore lacks agency.
- Even the dramatic events in the finale of the play are not brought about by his own actions but rather because of circumstance; for example, discovering that the sword is poisoned seems to prompt him to act.

Use in essays on...Action Vs Inaction; Morality; Revenge.

Edward P. Vining (1881) states,
> "The charms of Hamlet's mind are essentially feminine in nature."

Interpretation: Vining asserts that Hamlet's thoughts and emotions are those more commonly associated with females and therefore Hamlet is not a masculine character. This is supposed to go some way to explaining his inaction.

Analysis:
- "Charms" implies Hamlet's thoughts and emotions are favourable and advantageous to him. However, Hamlet's inaction often prevents him from confronting his problems directly and lead to his tragic downfall.
- So what are these "feminine" qualities? His essay goes on to say it is Hamlet's gentle nature and feigned madness that are his most feminine qualities. But what of Hamlet's anger, desire for revenge, and cruel treatment of Ophelia? Would Vining claim these more unpleasant aspects of his character are "masculine"? A modern audience would likely feel uncomfortable attributing gender stereotypes as an explanation for Hamlet's behaviour, but a Victorian audience would largely have had very fixed ideas about how men and women should act.
- This claim naturally leads us to consider Hamlet in the light of both Ophelia and Gertrude; what are their similarities and differences?

Use in essays on…Role of Women; Action Vs Inaction; Madness.

G.Wilson Knight (1930) makes the assertion that,
"Claudius…is not a criminal. He is…a good and gentle king, enmeshed by the chain of causality linking him with his crime."

Interpretation:
Knight claims Claudius is not the villain he is often said to be, arguing that the one crime he did commit trapped him in a difficult set of circumstances that led to his downfall.

Analysis:
- Initially it seems difficult to support an argument that so clearly contradicts itself. Knight claims Claudius is "not a criminal" yet qualifies this by saying he is trapped by "his crime". Perhaps Knight feels the label of "criminal" is more an aspect of someone's personality, rather than linked to a specific act. It is this we must decide – is Claudius inherently criminal or did he simply commit a crime?
- Claudius as a "good and gentle king" sits uneasily with his brother's murder and the plot to kill Hamlet. Could he be a good king but a bad man? He acts decisively with Fortinbras and creates peace between Denmark and Norway, but his actions ultimately lead to Norway taking over and the loss of many lives.
- Knight asserts Claudius is a victim of "a chain of causality", rather like Johnson claiming Hamlet is an instrument rather than an agent of his own destiny.

Use in essays on…Corruption; Morality; Appearance Vs Reality.

W.H.Clemen (1951) claims,
> "Hamlet sees through men and things. He perceives what is false."

Interpretation:

Clemen is praising what he sees as Hamlet's foresight and intuition about people, implying he cannot be fooled and is therefore a wise and honest man.

Analysis:

- If we accept this argument, we must accept the Ghost is truly King Hamlet's spirit - Hamlet is right to trust its message. Yet its appearance and all that follows brings nothing but tragedy; by the end of the play Hamlet seems to have forgotten him. We must therefore ask if Hamlet did eventually "see through" the ghost, or if he accepted the truth that his visitation was always going to end in death.
- Clemen clearly subscribes to the historical view of Hamlet as an intellectual hero capable of deep thought. Hamlet certainly sees through the foolish Polonius and Claudius' charm, but also ascribes more guilt to Gertrude than perhaps fair. Modern feminist readings often do not condemn Gertrude for marrying Claudius, believing her when she claims she knew nothing of the murder of King Hamlet.
- Hamlet also berates Ophelia harshly for lying to him, but it is commonly accepted that he knows her father is watching. Would a man who "sees what is false" not recognise the reasons behind her behaviour and be more forgiving?

Use in essays on... Appearance Vs Reality.

Maynard Mack (1952) observes that,
> "[Polonius] is always either behind an arras or prying into one."

Interpretation: Mack's metaphor states Polonius is a man who spends his life cultivating secrets, spying on private moments, or deceiving people he wishes to manipulate.

Analysis:
- This rather amusing analysis of Polonius' character does seem to sum him up rather well. From the moment he appears Polonius is sending his son off to university and at the same time planning to have him spied on. He not only intrudes upon Ophelia's private life (although one could argue an unmarried woman at this time did not have a life private from her father) but uses the details he learns to gain favour with the king.
- Polonius sees himself as a wise man, evident in his rambling speech to Laertes, yet he lacks the charm and rhetoric to manipulate others in the way Claudius does. Using Ophelia against Hamlet, hiring a spy for Laertes, and hiding behind tapestries are rather blunt, immature tools for gathering information.
- It is fitting that when Polonius is killed, Hamlet hides his body under the stairs, and his funeral is low-key and secretive. Polonius' characteristic hiding has followed him even into death.

Use in essays on...Appearance Vs Reality; Morality; Corruption.

Helen Gardner (1959) argues,
"The dark and devious world in which Hamlet finds himself…involves all who enter it in guilt."

Interpretation: Gardner is either suggesting those who participate in Hamlet's world are guilty by association with Claudius, or that Claudius has so infected the state of Denmark that immoral and corrupt behaviour have become commonplace.

Analysis:

- If "all who enter" Hamlet's world are guilty in some way then we must consider this in light of characters who seem to be the most innocent: Ophelia and Horatio. One could argue Ophelia allows herself to be used against Hamlet and is deliberately dishonest with him. Horatio, however, is a constant support and loyal friend to Hamlet, who does not implicate himself in any plots that fill the play.
- The constant plotting and scheming in the play certainly support Gardner's claim Hamlet lives in a "dark and devious world" and Shakespeare's language, filled with references to disease, death, and sin, contribute to a morbid, hopeless atmosphere.
- Is there something to be said for Hamlet "finding himself" in this unpleasant world? A literal reading could be Hamlet physically there, tied to the corrupt court. Yet, by the end we could claim Hamlet has indeed "found himself" by having to navigate this "dark and devious world", contemplate death, and reflect on who he truly is.

Use in essays on…Morality; Corruption; Revenge; Disease.

Rebecca Smith (1980) claims that,
> "[Gertrude] is caught miserably at the centre of a desperate struggle between two mighty opposites."

Interpretation: A great deal of pre-twentieth century criticism casts Gertrude in the same light as Hamlet and his father do; as a 'fallen' woman, guilty of adultery and/or incest. It is refreshing then, to consider a more sympathetic view of Gertrude as a woman struggling to find a balance between her roles as wife and mother.

Analysis:
- The claim Gertrude is caught "miserably" between Claudius and Hamlet is only explicit in the play when she learns Claudius killed King Hamlet. Many critics have decided Gertrude was likely to have had an adulterous relationship with Claudius prior to their marriage and so would assume she is happy with her choices. A more generous reading of this could lead us to consider her circumstances, having changed so dramatically, led her to marrying Claudius in an attempt to secure her future and save her son.
- A feminist reading of Gertrude finds her, like Ophelia, often silenced not only by her husband and son, but by Shakespeare himself. She is unable to assert herself until her final moments, when she defies her husband in order to toast (and warn?) her son. These warring "mighty opposites" lead her to death.

Use in essays on...Role of Women.

Elaine Showalter (1985) concludes that,
> "[Ophelia] is deprived of thought, sexuality, language."

Interpretation: Showalter is arguing that Ophelia is more of a plot device than a character. She has no agency and no control over the events that so badly affect her.

Analysis:
- In using "deprived" Showalter indicates these devices through which Ophelia may assert herself have been deliberately taken from her. We must conclude it is the men in her life who have starved her of the ability to think and speak freely.
- It is the sexuality aspect of Ophelia's character which is most interesting though. Laertes and Polonius police Ophelia's sexuality fiercely, but in so doing often reduce her to nothing more than an object to be desired. It is no surprise then, that after being rejected by her, Hamlet speaks to her in very explicit terms during the 'nunnery' scene and when they are watching the play. Ophelia, meanwhile, can do nothing but respond naively and politely.
- It is only during her madness that Ophelia can speak more freely, but even here she lacks the language to explicitly do so and can only express her sexuality through songs. She also uses the symbolic flowers to pass judgement on those around her; a bold act but still a limiting one.

Use in essays on...Role of Women; Appearance Vs Reality; Relationships and Sexuality.

Emma Smith (2019) makes the argument that,
> "[Hamlet] bears the name of a dead man. His very identity is caught up in the past."

Interpretation: Being named after his father, Smith believes that Hamlet is always destined to be trapped by the past, constantly looking back instead of looking forward.

Analysis:
- The Ghost calls on Hamlet to "remember me", immediately trapping Hamlet in a constant state of reflection and backwards glancing, worried that he is not avenging his father and obsessed with punishing those who have done him wrong. Hamlet's only moments of considering the future are those in which he contemplates death; either damnation for ending his own life or the reality of eventually turning to dust and clay.
- Smith expands her argument to state that it is ironic that a play often considered so modern in its understanding of the human psyche is one in which the antagonist spends so much time looking to the past. But perhaps this is the key to Hamlet's success; it is human nature to consider the past and reflect. Hamlet's behaviour therefore is not perverse or morbid, but that of a young man trying to make sense of the world.

Use in essays on... Disease; Madness; Revenge.

Performance History

When Puritans closed theatres 40 years after *Hamlet* was first performed, short theatrical performances called 'drolls' took to the stage. A popular droll, 'The Grave Makers', was adapted from Act Five. Rather than choose from the many soliloquys of Hamlet, audiences sought comic elements, with a focus on the grave diggers and their existential questions reflecting wider humanity, rather than political or familial themes. To audiences familiar with monarchical power struggles or familial battles for a throne, The Grave Makers focused on broader, more universal questions of life and death.

If audiences of the Puritan era wanted humour, the most explicit comparison would be David Garrick, the renowned Shakespearian actor, who cut the grave diggers, and indeed "all the rubbish of the fifth act", to place the focus almost exclusively on Hamlet's inner turmoil in his 1772 Drury Lane production. Garrick was a popular actor, perfectly placed to articulate Hamlet's personal internal chaos; what does it do to a production to omit the grave-diggers, Osric and the fencing match in the final act?

Many productions focus on Hamlet's individual suffering. In the 2017 Almeida Theatre production, with Andrew Scott as Hamlet, his suffering seems heavily focused on the loss of the family unit. Indeed, in Act 3 Scene 4, as Hamlet confronts Gertrude, he physically places her hand in the hand of his father's ghost, clasping them together in uncontrollable tears. Here, the driving force of the play is undoubtedly Hamlet's grief that he, his mother and father, no longer exist as a harmonious trio.

In terms of directorial choice there are numerous variations to explore. Women have played Hamlet for centuries; what does it do to interpretations of 'father-son' relationships, or to depictions of Gertrude or Ophelia? Modern interpretations can utilise CCTV on stage, with focus on the state of Denmark and the public sphere. Another choice concerns Hamlet's ghost; does it physically exist? Much like Banquo in *Macbeth*, if an actor plays the ghost, a physical connection is made; if the ghost remains simply a voice, or with today's technology, an image or hologram, how does it alter the thematic concerns of the play?

How to revise effectively.

One mistake people often make is to try to revise EVERYTHING!

This is clearly not possible.

Instead, once you understand the text in detail, a good idea is to pick five or six major themes, and four or five major characters, and revise these in great detail. The same is true when exploring key scenes – you are unlikely to be able to closely analyse every single line, so focus on the *skills* of analysis and interpretation and then be ready for any question, rather than covering the whole text and trying to pre-prepare everything.

If, for example, you revised Religion and Hamlet, you will also have covered a huge amount of material to use in questions about Corruption, Morality or Gertrude.

It is also sensible to avoid revising quotations in isolation; instead, bring together two or three textual quotations as well as a critical and contextual quotation so that any argument you make is supported and explored in detail.

Finally, make sure material is pertinent to the questions you will be set. By revising the skills of interpretation and analysis you will be able to answer the actual question set in the exam, rather than the one you wanted to come up.

Suggested Revision Activities

A great cover and repeat exercise – Cover the whole page, apart from the quotation at the top. Can you now fill in the four sections without looking – Interpretations, Techniques, Analysis, Use in essays on…?

This also works really well as a revision activity with a friend – cover the whole page, apart from the quotation at the top. If you read out the quotation, can they tell you the four sections without looking – Interpretations, Techniques, Analysis, Use in essays on…?

For both activities, could you extend the analysis and interpretation further, or provide an alternative interpretation? Also, can you find another quotation that extends or counters the point you have just made?

Your very own Quotation Bank! Using the same headings and format as The Quotation Bank, find 10 more quotations from throughout the text (select them from many different sections of the text to help develop whole text knowledge) and create your own revision cards.

Essay writing – They aren't always fun, but writing essays is great revision. Devise a practice question and try taking three quotations and writing out a perfect paragraph, making sure you add connectives, technical vocabulary and sophisticated language.

Glossary

Allusion – Referring to something in a sentence without mentioning it explicitly: biblical allusion to Cain killing Abel ("A brother's murder"), the first murder in the bible, stress that Claudius is aware of the severity of his sin.

Dramatic Irony – When the audience knows something the characters don't: at this moment Claudius must look as if he is praying and so he should be on his knees, looking as if he is begging for forgiveness. The audience, however, know this is not the case.

Imagery – Figurative language that appeals to the senses of the audience: Ophelia is often associated with flower imagery, and "violets" in literature are commonly associated with faithfulness, modesty, and chastity.

Irony – A statement that suggests one thing but often has a contrary meaning: ironically Laertes insists he "will not be juggled with" and will not be taken for a fool or manipulated. However, he allows himself to be led by Claudius who plots the murder of Hamlet in an underhand and deceptive manner.

Juxtaposition – Two ideas, images or words placed next to each other to create a contrasting effect: the juxtaposition of the adjectives "shameful" and "virtuous" not only describe Gertrude but also foreshadow Ophelia's downfall and the reasons why Polonius and Laertes warn her to stay away from Hamlet.

Language – The vocabulary chosen to create effect.

Metaphor – A word or phrase used to describe something else so that the first idea takes on the associations of the second: "Poison" being used to metaphorically describe the symptoms of grief could imply Claudius believes grief is a dangerous emotion and one that should be cured.

Motif – A significant idea, element or symbol repeated throughout the text: the repeated motif of "nothing" reminds us of Hamlet's desire to kill himself as he feels worthless.

Oxymoron – A figure of speech where apparently contradictory terms appear together: "noble dust" in reference to Alexander also brings to mind Hamlet's dead father.

Personification – A non-human object or concept takes on human qualities to make its presence more vivid to the audience: Hamlet believes women personify frailty, a weakness of body and mind, a typically misogynistic attitude of the period.

Repetition – When a word, phrase or idea is repeated to reinforce it: repetition of "Oh God, God" stresses Hamlet's pain and emotional torment over the death of his father.

Semantic Field – A group of words used together from the same topic area: the semantic field of religion stresses Laertes' determination for revenge, in contrast with Hamlet.

Simile – A comparison of one thing with something of a different kind, used to make a description more vivid: "Bosom black as death" conveys both guilt but also selfishness; he bemoans the darkness of his "bosom" as like death, yet he inflicted death upon his brother.

Soliloquy – A speech when a character talks to themselves: by talking about his "offence", this soliloquy takes the form of a confession or a prayer.

Acknowledgements:

Voltaire: *Dissertation sur la Tragédie* 1748
S Johnson: *Preface to Shakespeare* 1765
E P Vining: *The Mystery of Hamlet. An attempt to solve an old problem*, published by J B Lippincott & Co 1881
W H Clemen: *The Development of Shakespeare's Imagery,* published by Methuen & Co. Ltd 1951
G Wilson Knight: *The Embassy of Death: An Essay on Hamlet* from *The Wheel of Fire: Interpretations of Shakespearean Tragedy*, published by Oxford University Press 1930
M Mack: *The World of Hamlet,* published by *The Yale Review* Vol 41 1952
H Gardner: *The Profession of a Critic*, from a lecture given at University of London 1953
R Smith: *A Heart Cleft in Twain: The Dilemma of Shakespeare's Gertrude* in *The Woman's Part: Feminist Criticism of Shakespeare*, edited by C Lenz, G Greene, C Neely, published by University of Illinois Press 1980.
E Showalter: *Representing Ophelia: women, madness, and the responsibilities of feminist criticism* from *Shakespeare and the Question of Theory*, edited by P Parker and G Hartman, published by Routledge 1985
E Smith: *This is Shakespeare – How to Read the World's Greatest Playwright*, published by Penguin 2019.